Direct Current Voltage Gradient Surveyor
BASICS Reference Guide

Christien R. Stone - 2012

To better interpret the displayed voltmeter readings in the field and understand the flow of the current being logged and to be able to interpret DCVG data in combination with Close Interval Survey, this document will explain several of the more common phenomena encountered during surveys and what may help you determine quality data collection as opposed to simple contact problems revealing false faults/Potential Issues.

- The first thing to note before starting a DCVG survey is the calibration of the half cells to be used. A difference of more than five millivolts (or your company's allowable differences) between half cells should be rectified before starting the survey by cleaning the half cell(s) of greater difference(s) and re-readying them as is the norm. *Also note the for purposes of this manual Center Position is connected to positive while extremities are connected to negative to the extremity position surveyors' voltmeter.*

- Should one or both half cells to be used at the extremities of the survey reference a difference from the center half-cell of 1 to 5 millivolts, this should be noted so that the data may be compensated if needed, and so that readings in the field may be interpreted by the surveyor as actual when compensated after viewing the false readings displayed. For example, if the left hand side surveyor's half-cell is 5 millivolts more positive than the center surveyor's half-cell, his displayed Gradient readings will be five millivolts positive at zero, meaning 5 millivolts away from the pipe, and will display zero when there would actually be a reading of -5mV, meaning 5 millivolts towards the pipe. At this low range the effect would not be relevant when interpreting the collected data in order to find faults, dependent on exact Current being tested (potentially), but at the edge of the limit of company standards set at which to flag Possible Faults, it could make a difference in early fault detection, and confuse readings in which there is a Delta present. Combined with the used model handheld voltmeter's margin of error of up to four millivolts (individual differences will vary per unit), a 9 millivolt false reading could be confusing in the field if calibrations differences are not noted.

- To understand the displayed readings on voltmeters being used at the extremities of a DCVG survey you should be able to interpret the direction of flow of the current. By remembering that a positive reading signifies current moving away from the pipe, and a negative reading signifies current moving towards the pipe, you may be able to determine if your readings are accurate by plausibility, and if not plausible, you will be able to attend to the connection or contact problem prior to logging inaccurate readings. This directional interpretation is to be used when the center reference is connected in the positive terminal of the voltmeters used at the extremities. In the event that the center half-cell is connected in the negative terminal of the voltmeter, directional reference would have to be reversed.

To help understand it is sometimes beneficial to be able to visualize things we are trying to learn. It may help to draw out several scenarios with the current Flow/Path and Gradients in relation to the pipe.

Identifying a contact or connection problem

When a high Gradient is observed by a surveyor they should confirm that the readings are accurate and not a result of poor contact or connection issue. This can be accomplished by first making sure the ground the half-cell is resting in is not too dry and that no vegetation is present between the half-cell's contact with the ground which could be creating too high of a resistance for the voltmeter's rated impedance level (Our McMiller G1 is 400 Mega Ohms) creating false high Gradient readings as the voltmeter interprets the lack of current as such when the resistivity between the half cells exceeds 400 Mega Ohms. If the ground is too dry simply wetting the area under the half-cell may lower resistance enough to enable accurate readings to be achieved. Verify successful remedy of the issues by checking readings under varying impedance settings and confirming that reading change does not occur between two impedance levels, insisting that the voltmeter or setting being used has a higher circuit resistance than one which would alter/effect results.

If both surveyors' readings on the extremities have high readings, the center surveyor should also verify that they have good contact with the ground as the center half-cell affects both Gradients equally, and the half cells positioned at the extremities influence only themselves. (Possible *minor* influence to other Gradient half-cell in extremely poor conductivity soil conditions, up to 1 millivolt)

If connection problems are suspected with one surveyor's voltmeter, the surveyor outside of the effected instrument's circuit can place his half-cell directly beside the other surveyor's half-cell (simulating same circuit connections) and compare readings, keeping in mind any differences in half cell calibration and that the ground must be wet enough to have already eliminated contact problems. From there wire leads may be exchanged if the problem persists.

<u>Poor contact Example</u> *** accurate readings if foreign current was* *transferring to our pipe. But far more likely poor contact, verify the presence* *of pipe crossings*** (note current flow identical in directional reference to the pipe at both extremities ON AND OFF)

Left Hand Side
ON -0.033V   **OFF -0.034V**

Center (CIS if performing survey)
ON 1.785V   **OFF 0.987V**

Right Hand Side
ON -0.032V   **OFF -0.030V**

After contact has been verified and good contact established (readings within margin of error should there not be a Possible Fault in this section)

Left Hand Side
ON -0.001V   **OFF -0.002V**

Center (CIS if performing survey)
ON 1.785V   **OFF 1.008V**

Right Hand Side
ON -0.002V   **OFF -0.003V**

Noticing a Possible Fault

A section of pipe with a strong coating will generally be without or have very low Gradient readings. However, where there are Possible Faults, which may or may not actually be areas of low resistance on a section of pipe, Gradient will be present. Of which 5 or more millivolts accompanied by a Delta (the difference between the ON and OFF cycle readings) of 5 or more millivolts may represent a section of pipe where a Possible Fault is present.

Possible Fault Examples

Delta of 5mV with current towards the pipe in ON cycle and away from pipe in OFF cycle. (Possible small fault/holiday)

ON -0.004V   OFF 0.001V

Delta of 11mV with current towards the pipe in ON cycle and away from pipe in OFF cycle. (Possible fault/holiday)

ON -0.007V   OFF -0.004V

Delta of 61mV with current towards the pipe in the ON cycle and away from pipe in the OFF cycle. (Possible large fault)

ON -0.047V   OFF 0.014V

Less Obvious Possible Fault Examples

Delta of 5 with current towards the pipe in ON cycle (more negative ON) and away from pipe or not noticeable in OFF cycle, as the margin of error is 4mV plus or minus. **(Possible small fault)**

ON -0.008V   OFF -0.003V

Delta of 5mV with current possibly not flowing in this section in ON cycle (2mV within margin of error, and current may be flowing towards the pipe and entering through a path of lesser resistance up or down stream of this section) and away from the pipe in OFF cycle. **(Possible fault)**

ON 0.002V   OFF 0.007V

To determine whether or not readings are accurate and if there may actually be a Possible Fault, you should first notice if current is moving towards or away from the pipe in the ON cycle. If current is moving towards the pipe during the on cycle, this is correct, as the current would be flowing from our rectifiers ON cycle. If the current is moving away from the pipe during the ON cycle it is unlikely that this is a possible fault section being influenced by our rectifier. Cathodic and Anodic sections do exist within the same pipe sections where current may be read leaving the pipe in ON cycle, but are a rare occurrence; the first step would be to verify contact and connections.

High Gradient - Possible Foreign Influence or stray current

If the current is moving towards the pipe on one side and away from the pipe on the other side, it is likely that the voltage Gradient being read is simply current travelling over our pipe in an area of low resistivity soil and strong pipe coating or a foreign current path. However, a foreign current path could hide some of our pipe's voltage Gradient and Close Interval Survey's OFF pipe potential readings should be referenced to make sure our pipe potential is constant. For instance, if the ON Gradient on the left is 30mV and the OFF is 27mV both moving towards the pipe, foreign influence being read could be adding 25 millivolts towards the pipe to the readings, which would make the actual readings ON 5mV and OFF 2mV (2mV being within the margin of error), which would indicate a possible 5 millivolts towards our pipe influenced by our rectifier in the ON cycle. This could be confirmed if the Close Interval Survey's OFF potential has decreased within the area these high Gradients are observed. But compensating foreign influence readings may not always be an option as determining the source of foreign current can sometimes be difficult and unnecessary when combined with other survey methods.

With foreign influence read
(if displayed contact and connections should be verified)

Left Side Gradient

ON -0.030V   **OFF -0.027V**

Actual readings after compensation
(Displayed if influence were foreign and removed)

Left Side Gradient

ON -0.005V   **OFF -0.002V**

Stray current (foreign or not)

Small Delta, BUT current is moving away from the pipe with as much flow as it is moving towards the pipe on the opposing side. (4 millivolt margin of error and half-cell calibration differences should be taken into consideration).

Unlikely section to be influenced by Possible Fault, keep open communication with other surveyor.

Left Side Gradient

ON -0.012V   OFF -0.010V

Right Side Gradient

ON 0.014V   OFF 0.011V

Below - At first sight these high readings could indicate poor contact and or stray current, however in the ON cycle the current flow is higher towards the pipe form the left hand side and a lesser amount of current flow is moving away from the pipe on the right hand side in the ON cycle. Therefore current could be entering the pipe in this section. As well, the OFF cycle reading are more positive on both sides, revealing possible current loss from the pipe. If the center position is performing CIS and notices potential loss in the OFF cycle in this section there may be a Possible Fault present which could have appeared as stray current.

Left Hand Side

ON -0.043V   OFF -0.037V

Center (CIS if performing survey)

ON 1.786V   OFF 0.976V

Right Hand Side

ON 0.036V   OFF 0.039V

Gradient towards the pipe with no loss / separate entry and exit location

In areas with great differences in soil resistivity, Gradients may be observed accurately great distances away from areas of Possible Faults where the soil may be of very low resistivity in comparison to the actual area of a Possible Fault. This would occur as the current will travel the route of least resistance via vein of low resistivity soil, ditch, river or other, up to the pipe, and continue its path to a Possible Fault via the pipe. Thus generating high Gradient readings in the ON cycles towards the pipe on one or both sides (possibly falsely suggesting a Possible Fault), and possible CIS raised potential in the ON cycles, and no substantial Gradients in the OFF cycles. A section of pipe that maintains its OFF potential suggests there is no fault. The survey could then eventually lead to a section of pipe down the line where there will be Gradient away from the pipe in the OFF cycle accompanied by a CIS loss in pipe potential in the OFF cycle, although without a significant ON cycle Gradient, this would be the most likely section containing a Possible Fault.

Again, note that if there is positive Gradient on one side and negative Gradient on the other side the possibility of a foreign influence present may exist. However, by determining the Delta and directional reference of the Gradient you can determine how much current is actually moving towards the pipe from influencing rectifiers.

Most importantly, the section of pipe experiencing loss of current without signs of absorbing current should not be overlooked and may be less evident than most Possible Fault sections. Where this kind of occurrence would possibly generate readings like 4mV (or possible margin of error) ON and 6mV OFF, which would suggest the Delta of 2mV indicates no presence of Possible Fault, unless accompanied by pipe OFF potential loss by Close Interval Survey readings. Whereas, a standard Possible Fault section would be read with higher ON readings and share current readings moving away from the pipe in the OFF cycle. Keep in mind that larger areas of lowered resistance, Possible Fault areas, will generate greater Gradient and Delta readings and be easier to notice as they will generally not be subject to separate entry and exit location phenomena due to that fact that these areas are the path of less resistance.

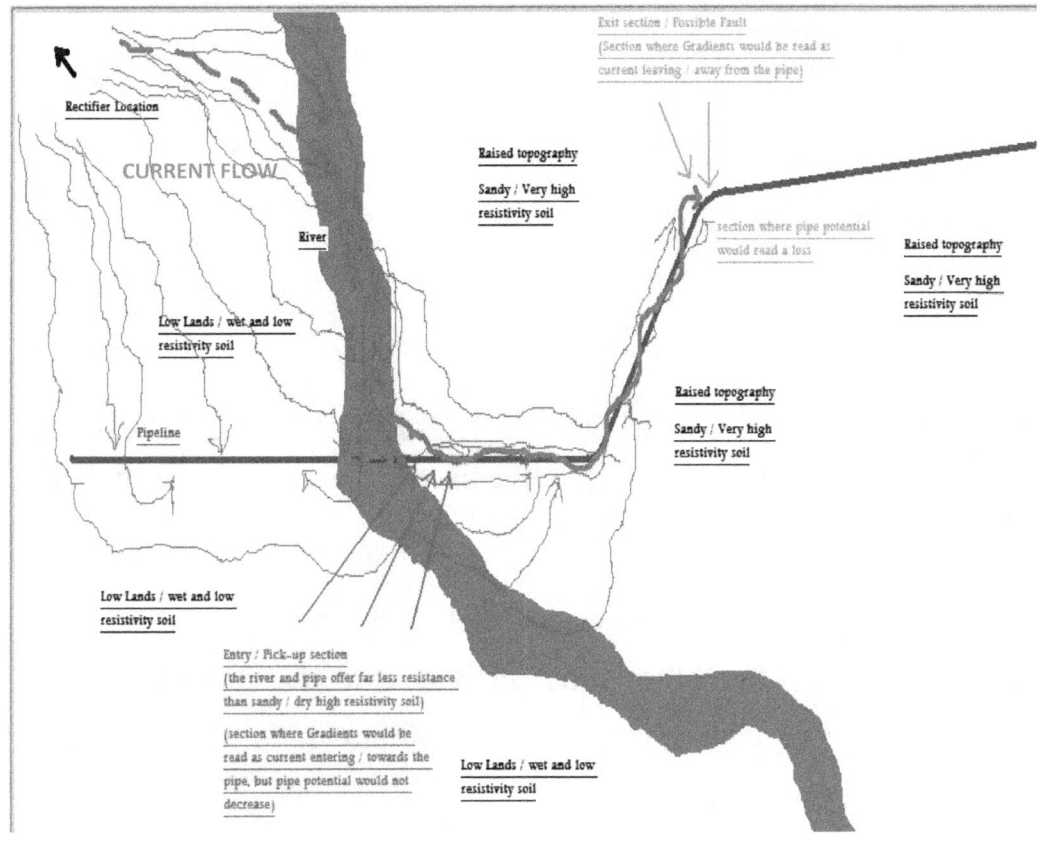

Rectifier Location

CURRENT FLOW

River

Raised topography

Sandy / Very high resistivity soil

Exit section / Possible Fault
(Section where Gradients would be read as current leaving / away from the pipe)

section where pipe potential would read a loss

Raised topography

Sandy / Very high resistivity soil

Low Lands / wet and low resistivity soil

Pipeline

Raised topography

Sandy / Very high resistivity soil

Low Lands / wet and low resistivity soil

Entry / Pick-up section
(the river and pipe offer far less resistance than sandy / dry high resistivity soil)

(section where Gradients would be read as current entering / towards the pipe, but pipe potential would not decrease)

Low Lands / wet and low resistivity soil

Above is a sketch of a possible current flow path with separate entry and exit locations. The following page illustrates possible readings that could be viewed during survey and demonstrates how actual low potential sections of the pipe may differ from high gradient sections. It is important to keep in mind past readings logged when surveying gradient with Close Interval Survey so that accurate data can be logged and faults may be flagged.

Observations of readings with separate entry and exit sections of current flow during DCVG and CIS survey (next chart)

Keep in mind there are always many variables, and reading from one extremity to the other may differ due to the location of the Possible Fault as well as soil resistivity fluctuations from one side of the pipe to the other.

Left Side Gradient			Center / CIS			Right Side Gradient		
ON	-0.003	3 meters	ON	1.877	3 meters	ON	-0.002	Current flow starting to enter
OFF	0.001	↓	OFF	0.978	↓	OFF	0.000	pipe, potential remains the same.
ON	-0.005	3 meters	ON	1.882	3 meters	ON	-0.004	
OFF	-0.001	↓	OFF	0.982	↓	OFF	0.000	
ON	-0.009	3 meters	ON	1.884	3 meters	ON	-0.005	
OFF	0.002	↓	OFF	0.980	↓	OFF	-0.001	
ON	-0.010	3 meters	ON	1.887	3 meters	ON	-0.005	Current flow entering the pipe
OFF	0.001	↓	OFF	0.977	↓	OFF	0.001	at vein of least resistance in ground.
ON	-0.006	3 meters	ON	1.888	3 meters	ON	-0.004	
OFF	-0.001	↓	OFF	0.979	↓	OFF	0.001	
ON	-0.003	3 meters	ON	1.885	3 meters	ON	0.001	
OFF	0.000	↓	OFF	0.982	↓	OFF	0.001	
ON	0.001	3 meters	ON	1.883	3 meters	ON	-0.002	
OFF	0.002	↓	OFF	0.974	↓	OFF	-0.001	
ON	0.002	3 meters	ON	1.884	3 meters	ON	-0.003	
OFF	0.002	↓	OFF	0.973	↓	OFF	-0.002	
ON	-0.002	3 meters	ON	1.881	3 meters	ON	-0.003	
OFF	0.004	↓	OFF	0.969	↓	OFF	0.003	
ON	-0.001	3 meters	ON	1.883	3 meters	ON	-0.002	
OFF	0.006	↓	OFF	0.956	↓	OFF	0.005	
ON	-0.001	3 meters	ON	1.880	3 meters	ON	-0.001	Current flow leaving the pipe
OFF	0.007	↓	OFF	0.953	↓	OFF	0.005	
ON	-0.002	3 meters	ON	1.878	3 meters	ON	0.001	
OFF	0.005	↓	OFF	0.970	↓	OFF	0.004	
ON	0.001	3 meters	ON	1.877	3 meters	ON	0.000	
OFF	0.003	↓	OFF	0.983	↓	OFF	0.002	

Recap and Conclusion, things to recognize during Surveys in order to maintain *Accurate* Data Readings

- Handheld voltmeter devices used to collect voltage readings are limited in their ability to detect voltage within a certain level of soil resistivity. This is the devices' impedance; this model of McMiller G1 had impedance rating of 400 Mega Ohms. This allows the device to provide accurate reading in reference to our current Copper Sulphate cells providing soil conditions are moist enough to provide an electrolyte of sufficient conductivity. Should readings be recognized as possibly implausible, the fore mentioned verification techniques should be used.

- The model McMiller G1 voltmeter used has a possible margin of error of 4 millivolts (individual voltmeter specifications should be consulted and recorded). Most survey situations will allow for this margin of error without affecting the integrity of the Data collected.

- Current flow readings will potentially fluctuate during surveys. In one survey position and in many. there are many paths for the flow of electricity to take and millivolts of electrical flow are constantly changing route in order to take the path of least resistance at all times. If an equipment or contact problem is suspected and eliminated, the possibility of actual fluctuation within Gradient readings does exist.

- Gradient readings of 20mV or more millivolts can be common in locating faults, but are also common in poor half-cell contact, especially when ON and OFF readings are both high and in the same directional reference, more commonly negative, to the pipe, due to arid soil conditions or foreign objects insulating between the half cell and the ground. If weather conditions are forecast to be hot during scheduled DCVG surveys water should be supplied and used to insure the best possible contact and least resistance between half-cell and ground. Foreign vegetation or debris should be removed from the surface of the ground before attempting to make contact with the ground.

- High Gradient readings common in Possible Fault/Holiday sections generally increase and then decrease gradually from one survey point to the next and are accompanied by a Delta.

- If Close Interval Survey is being performed in unison, pipe OFF potential can be very useful in confirming readings to ensure accurate Data is being collected. Should a surveyor be performing CIS they should be consulted during the survey at any time readings suggest anomalies by Gradient Surveyors. Should CIS not be performed, the center Surveyor should still be consulted as to whether their contact with the soil is good, and they should verify contact regularly in poor conditions as their half-cell influences both extremities.

DCVG surveys are generally completed with at least one experienced surveyor and they should be consulted at any time you may have a questions regarding. the equipment, readings, and start-up procedures using current software or any other topic you feel may influence your ability to Log accurate Data.